IMAGES
of America

AROUND COLUMBUS

Columbus, Texas, founded in 1835 and located along the Colorado River, is the county seat of Colorado County. It is conveniently equidistant from Austin, Houston, and San Antonio at the intersection of Interstate 10 and Highway 71. This c. 1910 photograph taken from the top of the Columbus Academy building shows the Colorado County Courthouse, the Stafford Opera House, and the city water tower with the steeple of the Methodist Church on the right. (Courtesy of Nesbitt Memorial Library.)

ON THE COVER: These bicyclists are participating in the Colorado County school fair in 1916 on the Colorado County Courthouse square. The bicyclists are, from left to right, Gladys Holt, Dorothy West, Willie Farrar Holland, Jocelyn Hamburger, Eva Mae Heller, Lavelia Kirby, and Mildred Goeppinger. (Courtesy of Nesbitt Memorial Library.)

IMAGES
of America

AROUND COLUMBUS

Roger C. Wade and Marilyn B. Wade

ARCADIA
PUBLISHING

Published by Arcadia Publishing
Charleston, South Carolina

Library of Congress Control Number: 2011938562

For all general information, please contact Arcadia Publishing:
Telephone 843-853-2070
Fax 843-853-0044
E-mail sales@arcadiapublishing.com
For customer service and orders:
Toll-Free 1-888-313-2665

Visit us on the Internet at www.arcadiapublishing.com

*This book is dedicated to the memory of Bill Stein, former director
and archivist of the Nesbitt Memorial Library in Columbus, Texas.*

CONTENTS

ACKNOWLEDGMENTS

This book would not have been possible without the foresight of Miss Lee Nesbitt to found the Nesbitt Memorial Library and archives and the efforts of Bill Stein to create what has been referred to as the best rural archives in Texas. Without Bill's love of history, most of the photographs included in this book, as well as thousands of other images of Columbus and Colorado County, would not have been preserved by the Nesbitt Memorial Library. Substantial portions of some of the captions used in this book are his descriptions of the photographs. The dedicated staff of the Nesbitt Memorial Library under the leadership of Library Director Nancy Koehl continues to improve access to materials in the archives. We also want to express our profound appreciation to Laura Ann Dick Rau, who has dedicated much of her life to preserving the history of Columbus, both privately and as executive director of the Columbus Historical Preservation Trust, Inc. Her reading of the manuscript has helped ensure its historical accuracy.

We would be remiss if we did not mention the Texas State University, San Marcos, public history faculty, headed by Dr. Lynn Denton, for the education they provided. Dr. Denton instilled in us concerns for "who owns the memory?" Katie Salzmann, archivist for the Wittliff Collection at the Alkek Library, provided superb training in archival procedures. We thank Dr. Donna Vliet for her sensitivity to engaging children in learning about their heritage, Dr. Peter Dedek for his enthusiastic love of historic preservation, and Tony Cherian for encouraging collaboration with others and the use of video interviews in public history projects.

Unless otherwise noted, all photographs are from the archives at the Nesbitt Memorial Library.

INTRODUCTION

Welcome to Columbus—the City of Live Oaks and Live Folks. Many of the largest live oaks in Texas are located in the Columbus area and have played an important role in our history, from shading the location of the first district court, to providing shelter for community gatherings in "the grove" and, on the darker side, serving as hanging trees. All of these events and more are explored in the following chapters.

Prior to formation as a city, the Columbus area was the site of several crossings of the Colorado River. The earliest of these was the Atascosito Crossing, located several miles south of Columbus, that was originally used by the Spanish in the 1700s. The Spanish also referred to the Atascosito Crossing as Montezuma. This was followed by Beason's Ferry in 1826 and DeWees Crossing around 1831, at what later became known as Columbus. The area was part of Stephen F. Austin's first colony, with original land grants being issued as early as July 7, 1824.

Rural Texas has always been a bastion of independent, patriotic souls, and Columbus is no exception. Citizens value their freedoms and have always been willing to fight to defend them. This has been evident even since before the Republic of Texas days.

During Texas's fight for independence from Mexico, Columbus was burned to the ground in what is known as "The Runaway Scrape." This event occurred as families fled in advance of Santa Anna's army in 1836. For several days, Santa Anna and the Mexican Army camped near Beason's Crossing on the west side of the Colorado River, and Sam Houston and the Texian Army camped on the east side of the Colorado River before retreating to the Brazos and ultimately San Jacinto. After the Texian victory at San Jacinto, the settlers returned to Columbus to rebuild. William Bluford DeWees and Joseph Worthington Elliot Wallace, the founders of Columbus, continued their development of the first platted Anglo community in present-day Texas. During the period of Texas independence, Columbus continued to grow rapidly with additional immigrants arriving from the southern United States followed by Germans coming directly from Europe.

The first real industry in the area was the opening of a German cigar factory in the 1840s. Tobacco soon gave way to cotton as a major crop for export outside the area. In 1860, Columbus was an agricultural center and in that year, Colorado County had the fifth largest cotton crop among Texas counties. The need for field labor resulted in the widespread use of slavery. With a total population of 7,885, there were 3,559 slaves.

In 1859, Alleyton, which lies just to the east of Columbus across the Colorado River, was formed as the result of an agreement between William Alley and the Buffalo Bayou, Brazos & Colorado Railroad (BBB&C) to share in the development of a town in return for extending the railway. During the Civil War, construction on the railroad was discontinued, and Alleyton became the terminus of the railroad. As a result of the blockade of Confederate ports, cotton from the South was shipped to Alleyton and transferred to ox-driven wagon trains, which then proceeded to Mexico on the "Cotton Road" to avoid the Union blockade.

After the Civil War as the railroads advanced to the west, the BBB&C became the Galveston, Harrisburg and San Antonio Railway, which purchased land three miles west of Columbus for new switching yards, a roundhouse, and maintenance shops to handle their increased traffic and additional traffic from the LaGrange Tap Railroad. This resulted in the creation of the town of Glidden in 1885. Glidden eventually became the largest Union Pacific Railroad maintenance facility between Houston and Los Angeles.

Reconstruction brought changes in government and some prosperity. During this period, two new courthouses were built and the Stafford Opera House was built in 1886. Justice, however, was uncertain, and citizens often took matters into their own hands, eventually resulting in the need for Texas Rangers to be assigned to Columbus on several occasions. This also resulted in the Stafford-Townsend and Reese-Townsend feuds that troubled the city for several decades. This violence was a great deterrent to growth in the area and resulted in the office of city marshal being abolished in 1903, followed by a vote to disincorporate the city in 1906. Columbus remained unincorporated until 1927. The population of Columbus had been 2,199 in 1890, but declined to 1,824 by 1900.

During the early 1900s, the local economy was also disrupted by the floods of 1913 and 1935, which destroyed homes, roads, and bridges. In addition, the flood of 1913 washed away many grave markers in the Old City Cemetery on the western edge of town. This has given rise to photographs purported to show ectoplasm in the haunted cemetery as a result of the disturbed souls.

The impact of World War I and II and the subsequent Korean, Vietnam, and Middle Eastern conflicts have also left their impacts on Columbus. Many volunteers from the Columbus area have offered their services in defense of our freedoms and some never returned. Those who did return have had an increased exposure to other cultures and nations. While the importance of agriculture to the local economy has declined during this period, oil discoveries have provided new employment and revenue sources for the local economy.

The role of religion has also been important in Columbus's development from early camp meetings and itinerant preachers to over 20 established churches in the area today.

Columbus's proximity to the ever expanding suburbs of Houston and increased access to internet technology have resulted in new opportunities for growth in the 21st century.

One

GONE TO TEXAS

The earliest known inhabitants of the Columbus area were members of the Karankawa and later the Tonkawa tribes of Native Americans. In January 1687, the first Europeans entered the area as part of the explorations of René-Robert Cavelier, Sieur de La Salle's—better known as Robert de LaSalle—which ended with his being killed by his own men. In 1690, the Spanish captain Alonso De León sought remnants of the French expedition in the area without success.

The first crossing of the Colorado River that was consistently used in the Columbus area was the Atascosito crossing south of Alleyton. The Spanish referred to this as Montezuma, and it was used by them to connect to the Spanish outpost of Atascosita in East Texas as early as the late 1700s and early 1800s. By the time of the 1823 census in the Colorado District of Austin's colony, there were 135 residents. In August 1823, Stephen F. Austin briefly contemplated establishing his capital at present-day Columbus, and with the assistance of surveyor Rawson Alley, even laid out a town. This made Columbus the first platted Anglo community in Texas. Austin later selected San Felipe as being safer from Indian depredations. This chapter explores the development of Columbus, Texas, from 1824 to the 1880s. During 1824, there were 24 land grants given in the Colorado District.

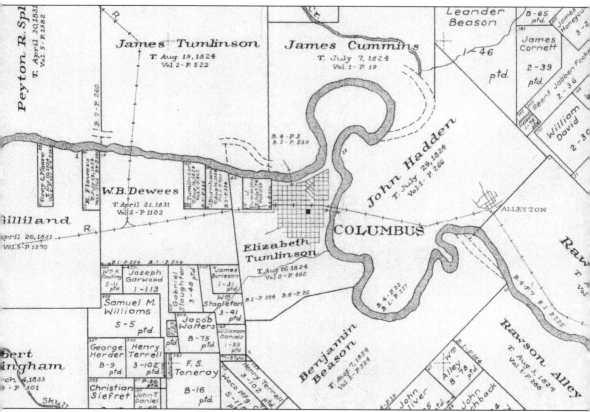

Elizabeth Tumlinson and Benjamin Beeson received two of the 24 land grants given in Stephen F. Austin's colony in 1824. Tumlinson was one of only three women to receive a land grant in that first year. In 1833, her land was divided into six lots and given to her six surviving children. Beeson's Crossing on the Colorado River was established by 1825 and was located somewhat closer to the current town of Columbus than the Atascosito Crossing. Other land grants in the Columbus area were given to William Bluford DeWees, James Tumlinson, James Cummins, John Hadden, and Rawson Alley. DeWees purchased a portion of Tumlinson's land in 1834 to establish DeWees Crossing. The first mention of the town being called Columbus occurred in December 1835, when it was designated as the seat of government for the new municipality of Colorado. The population was stated to be 1,500. Just a few months later, the war for Texas independence began. (Courtesy of Texas General Land Office.)

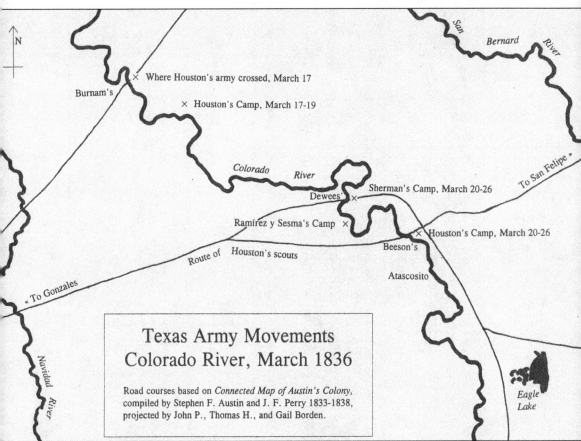

Texas Army Movements
Colorado River, March 1836

Road courses based on *Connected Map of Austin's Colony*, compiled by Stephen F. Austin and J. F. Perry 1833-1838, projected by John P., Thomas H., and Gail Borden.

After the Texans' defeat at the Alamo and the Runaway Scrape in late March 1836, Columbus was the site of a standoff between Texas Army general Sam Houston and Mexican Army general Joaquín Ramírez y Sesma. Houston had crossed the Colorado River at Burnam's Crossing and moved south to a position at Beeson's Crossing with smaller units at DeWees Crossing and the Atascosito Crossing. Many of the structures in the Columbus area were burned to the ground to avoid giving supplies and comfort to the Mexican Army during the Runaway Scrape. Houston considered fighting the Mexican Army at the Colorado River, but in the end retreated on March 26. Antonio López de Santa Anna arrived at the Mexican Army camp on April 4, and crossed the Colorado River at the Atascosito crossing on April 6. Santa Anna pursued Houston to San Jacinto, where the Mexican Army was defeated. After their defeat, the Mexican Army under Gen. Vicente Filisola and Gen. José de Urrea retreated and again crossed the Colorado River at the Atascosito Crossing in early May 1836.

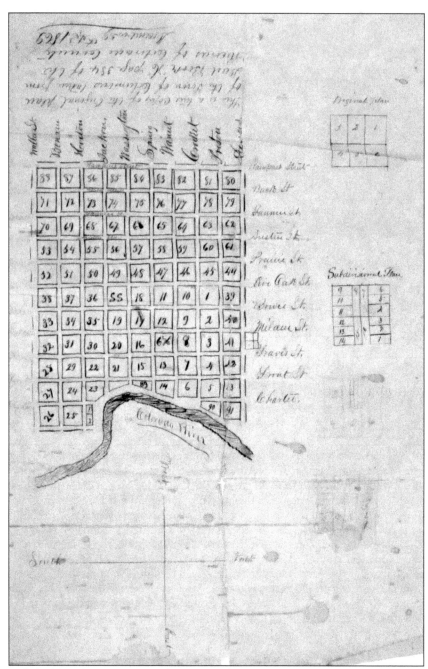

William Bluford DeWees was among the first residents to return to Columbus on May 10, 1836, after the Mexican defeat at San Jacinto and found most of the buildings destroyed. The rebuilding of Columbus began. The founding fathers of Columbus are considered to be the Tumlinson family and DeWees. Columbus is stated to have been the first platted Anglo community in Texas because Stephen F. Austin at one time contemplated establishing his capital at present-day Columbus and even went as far as having the town platted. When comparing this plat taken from the courthouse records in 1869 with maps of current Columbus, the route of the river has changed. Whether this was due to physical changes in the river or to earlier inaccuracies is not known.

William Bluford DeWees came to Texas in 1821 and married Benjamin Beeson's daughter Lydia in 1825. By 1840, his personal estate included 2,000 acres of land, 11 slaves, 30 cattle, 9 horses, and a carriage. In 1850, a book of his experiences, *Letters from an Early Settler of Texas to a Friend*, was published. He was justice of the peace and county treasurer. In 1866, his fortunes changed; he was convicted of misappropriating $1,200 of county funds. He died a poor man.

Benjamin Beeson was one of Austin's "Old 300." Beeson's Crossing was used from 1822 to 1836; he established the first ferry in the Columbus area. He and his family were part of the Runaway Scrape in 1836, and he died in early 1837. His daughter Mary Ann, pictured here, was born in 1829.

13

Dilue Rose, the daughter of Dr. Pleasant Rose, arrived in Texas in 1833 at the age of eight. The family settled in Harrisburg. In 1836 at the age of 11, she had melted lead in a pot and molded bullets for soldiers at the Alamo. Following the fall of the Alamo, her family fled from their home by oxcart during the Runaway Scrape. She moved with her husband, Ira Harris, to Columbus in 1845. Later in life she wrote of her experiences; the work was entitled "Reminiscences of Dilue Rose Harris" and was published in the *Quarterly of the State Historical Association* in the early 1900s. This is a picture of her home from 1906 with Placide and Eva Braden Heller, the owners at that time, in the yard. Her concrete-constructed home in Columbus was built in 1858 and is currently under the care of the Columbus Historical Preservation Trust, Inc.

Towns around Columbus were founded based upon connections to the railroad. Alleyton was founded in 1860 by William Alley, who owned the land in partnership with the Harrison family, who committed to opening a general store and the Buffalo, Bayou and Brazos Railroad, which committed to establishing a railhead. William Alley was one of Austin's "Old 300." This picture is of Nancy Millar Alley, who married William's brother Abraham in 1835 and lived in the cabin that William and his brothers built.

The original Alley cabin was built by Rawson Alley at the Atascosito crossing. It was destroyed during the Runaway Scrape in 1836 and was rebuilt later that year by William and Abraham Alley. It is in a Midwestern style with square notched corners. In 1976, the cabin was moved by Abraham Alley descendents to Bowie Street in Columbus, where it remains under the care of the Columbus Historical Preservation Trust, Inc.

In 1881, the Galveston, Harrisburg and San Antonio railroad company moved its roundhouse and shops to a new site three miles west of Columbus, now known as Glidden. The site was originally part of the William Bluford DeWees land grant. The railroad owned the land in the area, platted the town, and constructed a store and a hotel. This photograph shows the turntable at the Glidden roundhouse with the town in the background.

Two

River Crossings and the Sunset Route

The Columbus area has always been an important transportation hub, and the original river crossings on the Colorado River were the first important transportation routes. The Atascosito Crossing across the Colorado River south of Columbus was used originally by the Spanish; Beeson's and DeWees Crossings were used by early settlers, and both figured prominently in the Texas War for Independence from Mexico.

A stage line began operation in 1839 on a route from Houston to Columbus. In 1847, it continued west to San Antonio. In 1860, the Buffalo Bayou, Brazos & Colorado Railroad, the first railroad in Texas, came to Alleyton. It was to this route that the moniker "the Sunset Route" was first applied because it took from sunrise to sunset to travel from Buffalo Bayou to Alleyton. The first railroad bridge into Columbus was erected in 1867. It spanned the Colorado River on the east side of town.

The first road bridge across the Colorado River on the north side of Columbus was built in 1875. In 1886, an east bridge was established, although ferries were still used during periods of high water. With the arrival of motor vehicles came paved roads. By the 1920s, US Highway 90 was completed and in the 1960s, Interstate 10 was built along a similar route giving speedier access to both Houston to the east and San Antonio to the west.

In 1845, the *Kate Ward* was the first steamboat to operate on the Colorado River, and in 1846, it went from Matagorda on the coast to Austin. It was able to carry 600 bales of cotton with a draft of three feet. Its last recorded use was in 1853. Part ownership was attributed to a Mr. Robinson of Columbus, but most likely it was Robert Robson, a Scotsman who had built a concrete castle on the Colorado River in Columbus. The castle was complete with running water, a ballroom, a roof garden, a moat, and drawbridge. It is said that guests from Bastrop to Matagorda attended parties held there, which would have been very convenient for someone who owned a steamboat. The foundation was undermined by a flood in 1869. The boat shown in the photograph is thought to be the *Moccasin Belle*, one of two smaller steamboats to ply the Colorado River. The anchor from the *Moccasin Belle* is enshrined on the front lawn of the Tait House in Columbus, as steamboats stopped at Tait's Landing, south of Columbus.

Starting in 1847, stagecoach lines provided mail and passenger service between rural communities. Later, railroad connections and the arrival of the automobile made transportation easier. Multiple stage coach lines provided service from Columbus to San Antonio in the west, Eagle Lake to the east, and La Grange to the north. This photograph of a Concord-style stagecoach that was used in Texas was taken at the Columbus Quincentennial celebration on the courthouse square in 1992. The Stafford home and Opera House can be seen in the background. Carol Helms is in the stagecoach owned by Jimmy Helms, and the team of horses was provided by the Strunks of Oakland, Texas. (Courtesy of Jimmy Helms.)

In 1859, the Buffalo Bayou, Brazos & Colorado Railroad came to Alleyton. As the terminus of the railroad, Alleyton became a critical point in the shipping of cotton to Europe during the Civil War. With Texas ports blockaded by the North, cotton was shipped by rail from East Texas and Louisiana to Alleyton, where it was transferred to wagons and oxcarts and carried on the cotton road from there to Matamoras, Mexico. This facilitated the continuation of cotton exports to Europe in return for much needed military supplies. In 1867, the Columbus Tap Railroad was completed across the Colorado River into Columbus. This photograph from the early 1900s shows the second story of the Columbus depot being removed.

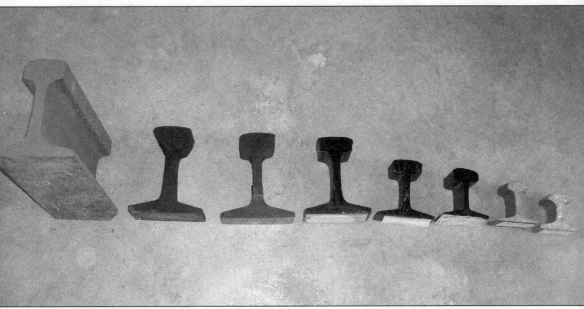

The cross sections of rails shown in this photograph provide a complete history of the rails used on the Buffalo Bayou, Brazos & Colorado Railroad from 1859 (right) to its current status as the Union Pacific Railroad (left). The rail on the far right weighs 36 pounds per three feet; the current rail on the left weighs 138 pounds per three feet. The cross-section of the rails start out symmetrical, but over time, the wheel flanges wear down the head on one side. If this wear becomes pronounced, the rails are reversed in order to double their useful life. The earliest rail on the right is made of iron. The others are steel. (Courtesy of Dittman Harrison.)

The photograph above shows locomotive 595(3), sidetracks, and railroad men at Glidden. By 1891, Glidden became the largest maintenance facility between Houston and Los Angeles for the Union Pacific Railroad. As seen below, the size of the station and the landscaping indicate the importance of the Glidden station. Trains from Houston passed through the Glidden junction on their way to either San Antonio or north on the LaGrange Tap Railway. With the advent of diesel engines and the passing of steam engines, the facilities became obsolete and were reduced to switching yards in the 1950s.

The North River Wagon Bridge was built in 1874 as a toll bridge across the Colorado River by the Columbus Iron Bridge Company. It was purchased by Colorado County and made a free bridge in 1884. It was the first non-railroad bridge across the Colorado River in the Columbus area. Thomas B. Elrod took this photograph in 1884 for exhibition at the New Orleans World Exposition.

The first railroad bridge was constructed in 1867 by the Columbus Tap Railway, when railroad construction resumed in the South after the Civil War. It was located between Crockett and Walnut Streets. The ferry was operating at the bottom of Crockett Street, which is believed to be the site of DeWees Crossing.

The East River Wagon Bridge is shown under construction in 1884 at the foot of Spring Street in Columbus. This photograph is one of a set of 20 that was made in Columbus in 1884 by Thomas B. Elrod and sent for exhibit to the New Orleans World Exposition. On December 4, 1884, *The Colorado Citizen* referred to the photograph as "Construction of Free Bridge." It collapsed in 1928 under the weight of a tractor and grader, and one man was killed.

The automobile greatly expanded the horizons of local travel and more closely tied Columbus to surrounding cities. The freedom to travel without worrying about train schedules or having to rest and feed horses greatly increased the exposure of rural residents to newer innovations and styles and facilitated travel among local communities. The group above is on a local outing around 1925, and includes Dorothy West as a child standing on the running board of the rear car. Her mother, Irma, is visible over her left shoulder. George Gegenworth is the man between the cars.

In this photograph from around 1925, Willis Evans Adam is the man in the dark suit leaning on the spare tire. The other men are unidentified.

This photograph shows old US Highway 90 where it runs between Columbus and Alleyton. It formed part of the Old Spanish Trail that ran from St. Augustine, Florida, to San Diego, California. It is of single-slab concrete construction, which was common for concrete roads in the 1910s and 1920s. This is one of the few locations where the original single-slab 17.5-foot wide concrete pavement can still be seen. When a newer, higher bridge for US Highway 90 was built in 1939 to avoid the frequent flooding, this section of road was bypassed. The new Highway 90 itself became less used with the coming of Interstate 10 that connects Columbus with Houston and San Antonio. As with the railroads and local roads before it, the construction of Interstate 10 in the 1960s greatly affected development in Columbus. New commercial development tended to focus around Interstate access, resulting in new motels, gas stations, and restaurants at both the Columbus exit and, to a lesser extent, the Alleyton exit.

Three

Nature on Display

Columbus, like any other town on a river and relatively close to the coast, has not been immune to the natural disasters of floods and hurricanes. The Colorado River that flows on the north and east sides of Columbus has recorded over 80 major floods since the early 1800s. Major floods in 1833, 1843, 1852, 1869, 1900, 1913, 1922, and 1935 caused damage to the towns all along the Colorado River. Columbus did not escape their rampages. The dams built on the Colorado River in the 1930s helped alleviate the flooding problem, but floods during the 1990s caused damage to ranch and farm land along the river above and below Columbus. An extended El Niño in December 1991 caused rains totaling 12 to 16 inches in the Hill Country. Lake Travis near Austin was pushed to its all-time high of 710 feet, which was within four feet of the top of Mansfield Dam. Extensive flooding was the result downstream.

While the river could be partially controlled by dams upstream, hurricanes cannot be controlled at all. Texas and, to some extent, Columbus were buffeted by hurricanes on numerous occasions. The most notable were the unnamed storms in 1875, 1900, and 1909 and Carla and Beulah in 1961 and 1967, respectively. The storm that made landfall in Galveston in 1900 caused massive damage to that town and continued inland to cause losses in Columbus as well. The storm of 1909 blew the clock tower off the Colorado County courthouse. When Hurricane Carla came ashore in September 1961, it brought a lot of wind and rain, and to Columbus, it brought refugees from the coastal areas. Columbus housed and fed the refugees for several days until they could return to their homes closer to the coast.

Fire has also taken its toll on the area around Columbus. A fire that was not natural and solely the fault of man occurred northeast of Columbus on the Fourth of July in 2010. It was caused by a group of people shooting off fireworks during a drought. After these disasters, Columbus was able to resiliently rebuild its businesses, houses, and bridges.

Recurring floods along the Colorado River led to the formation of the Lower Colorado River Authority (LCRA) in 1934 and the building of the Mansfield Dam near Austin. The dam was named for Joseph Jefferson Mansfield, a Columbus resident, who represented the Ninth Texas Congressional District in the US Congress. Mansfield served on the House River and Harbors Committee and became chairman in 1931. He was responsible for securing federal funding for the dam project in Austin. During this flood in September 1900, the railroad bridge on the east side of Columbus that connected the town to Houston was partially destroyed. In this photograph, trains can be seen on both sides of the bridge. This flood occurred later in September and was not the result of the category four hurricane that hit Galveston on September 8, 1900. This flooding was caused by the more than 11 inches of rain that fell in North and Central Texas. The Brazos and Trinity Rivers were also flooded by this same weather system.

The flood of December 1913 was one of the worst and caused the Brazos and Colorado Rivers to merge below Columbus, forming a 65-mile-wide lake. The flood was caused by a slow moving winter storm after a wet autumn and earlier flooding along the Colorado in October 1913. It started at the upper Colorado River on December 1 and worked its way down to the Columbus area a few days later. At that time, there were no dams upstream on the Colorado River; consequently, there was no flood control. The photograph above shows the wagon bridge on the east side of Columbus in December 1913 before the bridge washed out. The photograph at right shows the same bridge after it was washed out by the flood waters. This was the bridge that connected Columbus to Alleyton and Houston.

The photograph above of the Hotel Colorado, taken on the morning of December 5, 1913, after the floodwaters had hit Columbus, shows a man believed to be Walter Gresham Dick in a canoe offering help to four women and a young boy on the porch of the hotel. The photograph below was taken the same morning and is looking north on Milam Street from Crockett Street. It was taken well before the flood waters receded, since the Colorado River did not crest until the next day at 44.1 feet. This was 20 feet above flood stage. The photographer for both images is identified as Ashmore.

The Zwiener house, near the southwest corner of Second Avenue and Milam Street in Columbus, is shown here during the devastating flood of 1913. The floodwaters are halfway up the fence and have almost reached the porch. The *Weimar Mercury* reported on December 12 that the Colorado River was at 44 feet at Columbus. Normal flood stage was 24 feet.

These houses, located on the west side of Columbus, were moved off of their foundations by the flood. The street that runs in front of them turned into a creek that eroded the foundations of the houses, causing the damage. The photographer identified as Ashmore took this photograph on December 8, 1913.

This photograph from the 1913 flood shows an unknown man standing on the railroad tracks next to a telegraph pole almost completely submerged. The photograph is captioned "Will we ever use them wires again. Columbus, Tex Dec 8 '13." On December 12 of that year, the *Weimar Mercury* reported that the river had risen so high that Columbus was surrounded by water and that this flood dwarfed the historic flood of 1869.

The same flood that caused damage in Columbus also affected Glidden. This group of men is seen standing on the railroad tracks next to telephone poles, half covered with floodwaters. Residents of Columbus were brought west to Glidden in boxcars pulled by a switch engine from Glidden. The floodwaters eventually ate away the dirt under the tracks, which snapped under the strain.

Alleyton, on the east side of the Colorado River, was also affected by the December 1913 flood that devastated Columbus. The track between Alleyton and Columbus, as well as the railroad bridge that crossed the Colorado River, sustained damage. Here it can be seen that the floodwaters almost covered the platform of the Alleyton Depot. The depot was located near the railroad line at Center Street.

This home in Alleyton, located at the corner of Bond and Ross Streets (now Old Alleyton Road and Canal Street, respectively) and owned by Berthold Leysaht, had floodwater damage on the first floor. The owners can be seen on the second floor balcony watching the floodwaters as they flowed past their house. This photograph was taken on December 6, 1913, before floodwaters had receded.

The *Colorado County Citizen* reported in May 1922 that "water undermined the pier on this end of the [north] bridge, and when it gave way, the first span went with it." A ferry was initially put in place to allow traffic to cross the river. The floodwaters also destroyed crops on approximately 6,000 acres of farmland, causing hardship for the farmers who were without resources to replant.

According to William Henry Harrison's journal about the flood of 1935, word was received on Saturday, June 15, that "the river was roaring southward from Marble Falls with a wall of water exceeding that of the 1913 rampage." This photograph shows the East River Bridge and the railroad bridge during the 1935 flood. Because of the extensive damage during the 1913 flood, these bridges were watched closely.

These boaters are identified as, from left to right, Laura Glithero, ? Sronce, Lillian Sronce, and Susie Sronce. The floodwaters hit Columbus early in the morning on Tuesday, June 18, 1935. According to the *Colorado County Citizen*, most of the damage to houses was on the west side of town. Total damage to Columbus was estimated at $724,000.

These canoers were photographed on June 19, 1935, near Sidonia Auerbach's house in Columbus. According to William Henry Harrison's journal, "Highway patrolmen were in charge of the bridges at Columbus and were keeping the traffic as light as possible. Crews were busy removing drift logs from the piers of both the railroad and highway bridges."

This photograph shows the intersection of Fannin and Walnut Streets where the Horn Palace was located; it was a combination grocery store and gas station run by William B. Martin. The river eventually crested at a little over 38 feet, just shy of the 40 to 41 feet that was predicted. This photograph was taken on June 18, 1935.

These two men with a boat were photographed in front of Davis Drug Store. The flood affected those farther down the river as well. According to William Henry Harrison's journal about the 1935 flood, "the Everett Store [in Alleyton] was crowded all day with people getting relief supplies and enough provisions to carry out with them. Mr. [Cunningham Leroy] Griffith worked all day checking out groceries to the needy families."

On the north side of Columbus, the highway goes under the railroad track close to the Colorado River. This is a photograph of that underpass completely filled with floodwater from the 1935 flood. The photographer is facing south towards Columbus. Fortunately, there was ample notice of the flood, so precautions could be taken and no lives were lost in the Columbus area.

According to the *Colorado County Citizen* in June 1935, "a large force labored all day Sunday and Sunday night, and remained on picket duty through Monday as the water rose here from a low stage of 10 feet Saturday to 26 feet Sunday evening and a gradual rise from then until the high stage was reached at 6:00 p.m. Tuesday, the gauge standing at 38.18 at six and seven thirty."

While the same storm that hit Galveston Island in 1900 moved inland to Columbus, the town did not suffer the damage that was bestowed on Galveston. On the other hand, the storm of 1909 removed the clock tower of the courthouse and caused much damage to the jail. These photographs show the Colorado County Courthouse before the storm of 1909. The *Weimar Mercury* went on to report that "the commissioners should remember the people are in poor shape at the present time to bear additional burdens in the way of taxation, possibly rendered necessary in case the repairs are of too expensive character . . . and with losses to every citizen of the county through storm damage, make the burden as light as possible. Repair, but be as economical as possible about it."

After the 1909 storm blew off the tower of the courthouse, a new roof was constructed. Instead of rebuilding the tower as it was, it was replaced with a dome, and the roof profile was revised to the current configuration. According to the *Colorado Citizen*, "the bell that tolls the hour of time was carried to the west and completely buried in the ground near the well. The cornice and slate was blown down from the roof in several pieces and the rain nearly all night poured its volume into the wrecked court house completely saturating almost every room causing the plastering to fall off the walls." In addition to the damage done to the courthouse, the jail had several windows damaged and sections of the roof were torn off.

In July 2009, while a burn ban was in effect for Colorado County because of a severe drought that hit the area, a family decided to set off fireworks that ignited grass and brush north of Alleyton near a heavily wooded area. The result was the worst fire that Colorado County has ever seen. An estimated 1,804 acres were burned, and it took several days to completely extinguish the fire. Fortunately, no lives were lost, but several houses and vehicles were destroyed. The photograph at left shows the fire from a distance raging behind a barn. The bottom photograph shows one of the fire breaks created by the firefighters and a flat bottom boat left on the shore of a small pond that was crumpled by the heat of the fire. (Authors' collection.)

Four

MAYHEM IN COLUMBUS

Early settlements in the West were characterized by violence and lawlessness. Columbus was no exception to this mayhem. From early deaths in Indian conflicts through the Texas War for Independence, reconstruction after the Civil War, and the lack of an effective impartial system of justice in the late 1800s and early 1900s, death by violence was not uncommon. In the summer of 1824, Alcalde John Tumlinson and an associate were attacked by a party of Waco Indians, and Tumlinson was killed. It is on his land grant that Columbus is formed. In 1823, John Alley was killed by Indians and in 1826, Thomas Alley drowned after falling off his horse while chasing Indians. It was John and Thomas's brother William Alley who later founded Alleyton. These events foretold violent deaths that occurred to several subsequent community leaders. Later events were also related to cattle rustling, discrimination against blacks, and feuds. In particular, the Stafford-Townsend and Townsend-Reese feuds and the accompanying violence received sufficient notoriety to bring in the Texas Rangers under Capt. Bill McDonald. During an overlapping time frame, the Ku Klux Klan was active during the 1860s and later again in the 1920s. In addition, the Glidden ax murder achieved national notoriety.

The Glidden ax murder took place on the night of March 26, 1912. Lyle Finucane was employed by the Galveston, Harrisburg & San Antonio Railroad and worked in the Glidden roundhouse. He worked until midnight and then went to the home of Ellen Monroe, with whom he lived. Sometime during the night, they and four of Monroe's children were killed. In the morning, another daughter discovered the bodies and the murder weapon—an ax from the family's own woodpile. There were a series of ax murders in Louisiana and Texas resulting in 49 deaths during the period from January 1911 to April 1912. No one was ever convicted of the crimes. The photograph, which was taken by Oscar Zumwalt, shows the home in which the murders occurred and many of the victims' neighbors.

"Colorado Co. Protects 'Womanhood'" is the caption. This photograph shows the bodies of Bennie Mitchell and Ernest Collins, victims of a lynching, suspended from "the hanging tree." In October 1935, a white woman named Geraldine Kollmann was found face down in Cummins Creek. Two black male teens were questioned and, within a day, arrested for the murder of Kollmann. After long hours of questioning, they were forced to confess to the murder. Because the two were under 18, the law would prohibit the death penalty. They were taken to Houston for their safety and returned about a month later for the court hearing. The two were snuck back into Columbus the night before the trial. The officers transferring the teens were stopped by an armed mob of white men and forced to surrender them. The teens were driven away and the officers were left behind. The boys were taken to the area where Kollmann's body was found and hanged. This photograph is representative of the time in which it was created, but many do consider it to be offensive by current standards.

Bob Stafford, Asa Townsend, and Shanghai Pierce were cattle owners who shared open range in the area south of Columbus after the Civil War. Stafford ended up feuding with both Townsend and Pierce over cattle and wire fencing. The Townsends' strength was in politics and the Staffords had great financial success. The Pierce ranch at one time consisted of over half a million acres. Illicit branding was so common that vigilante groups were formed to try and stop the practice. Pierce and Stafford prevented physical conflict by avoiding each other. Such was not the case for the Staffords and Townsends. The first bloodshed occurred in 1871, when Sumner Townsend and Ben Stafford had a gunfight in which Ben was shot in the ankle, and Sumner was seriously wounded in the arm and shoulder. This 1884 photograph shows Bob Stafford and his house.

On July 7, 1890, a celebration was held with the laying of the cornerstone for the new Colorado County Courthouse. In the early part of the day, Columbus City marshal Larkin Hope (a kinsman of Sheriff Light Townsend) had taken Bob Stafford's son Warren to the calaboose for being drunk. After the laying of the cornerstone, Bob Stafford and his brother John confronted both Larkin and Marion Hope in front of the Nicolai Saloon about the arrest of Warren. This resulted in the shooting deaths of both Bob and John Stafford. There was some speculation that the argument had been engineered by Light Townsend. This painting by Ken Turner shows a scene from that fateful day with Bob Stafford's widow in the white dress. (Courtesy of Ken Turner.)

Sheriff James Light Townsend (known as Light) was a son of Asa Townsend. When he was elected sheriff, there were house burnings and cattle rustling in the area. In an effort to stop the mayhem, as one commentator said, "he begin to whittle 'em down, kill 'em out, one at a time. He never killed nobody; he'd have it done. Ol' man Light never killed a man." Light Townsend hired his son-in-law Larkin Hope and Samuel Reese as deputies. In 1880, Light Townsend was elected sheriff and the family moved to the city jail. In 1894, he was reelected as sheriff six days before his death, but he was seriously ill at the time and never knew it. The same commentator said, "ol' man Light got sick and died at his house, with his boots on. He didn't get killed."

Larkin Secrest Hope was no stranger to mayhem. In 1879, he was charged by the state of Texas with assault with intent to murder. A man named Burton had followed him across a field in what Hope regarded as a threatening manner. Later, Larkin Hope and Samuel Reese were deputies of Sheriff James Light Townsend and in March 1894 arrested some tramps who had stolen a boat and clothing, pocketknives, and tobacco from the Hahn store in Columbus. This led to Oscar Zumwalt's apocryphal story that the tramps, being unfamiliar with the area, stole a boat near the north bridge and made their getaway down the Colorado River. Downriver 14 miles, they saw two bridges and abandoned their boat only to be arrested by Hope and Reese at a point about half a mile from the scene of the crime. As can be seen on the map in chapter one, there is a large ox bow in the Colorado River at Columbus. This photograph shows Larkin Hope wearing the hat in which he was killed in an ambush by Jim Coleman in 1898.

Another colorful Columbus resident was Ike Towell. He was sheriff of Columbus and brought Jim Crow laws to Columbus in the late 1800s, when he segregated the waiting rooms at the train depot into one for whites and one for blacks. This cost him the next election for sheriff as the blacks then voted for his opponent Larkin Hope, and Towell was put out of office. After suffering a stroke about a year before his death, he had a tombstone erected with the epitaph: "Here rests Ike Towell—An infidel who had no hope of heaven nor fear of hell, was free of superstition, to do right and love of justice was his religion." Shortly before his suicide, he went into a local barbershop for a 50¢ haircut and asked, "How much do you charge to shave a dead man?" The response was $2. "Well I just saved a dollar and a half." According to one wag, his death certificate reportedly said he died of chloroform applied by Towell.

Samuel Houston Reese was the Colorado County sheriff from 1894 to 1898. As with many law enforcement officers at that time, it is uncertain whether they were a calming or disruptive influence on society. In 1890, Sam Reese participated in the shooting of Bob and John Stafford on Milam Street next to the courthouse. In the sheriff's race of 1898, Larkin Hope ran against Reese, the incumbent. When former Texas state senator Mark Townsend put his support on Hope, feelings ran high. Larkin Hope was shot and killed by Jim Coleman, an associate of Reese's, on the streets of Columbus prior to the election. Hope was immediately replaced by Will Burford who, with Townsend's support, won the election. On March 16, 1899, Mark Townsend, Will Clements, and Marion Hope, brother of the dead Larkin Hope, engaged Sam Reese and his supporters in a gunfight in downtown Columbus. Reese was killed. This photograph shows Reese in the 1890s.

Accidents also took their toll on the citizens of Colorado County. In February 1928, a section of the East River Wagon Bridge collapsed under the weight of a tractor and grader; one man was killed. William Henry Harrison recalls crossing the bridge to school just before the collapse and spending a long time getting home to Alleyton that evening by way of the North Bridge and the Cummins Creek Bridge. In the photograph at left, Alleyton residents Lillie Leeseman and Annabel Neal Everett are shown on the left part of the bridge inspecting the damage. The automobile accident pictured below in May 1958 was on Highway 90 near Glidden, in which John and Conradina Reimers of Weimar were killed. This photograph was originally printed in the *Weimar Mercury* on May 26, 1958.

Five

LAW AND ORDER RESTORED

Law and order started early in the Columbus area with circuit judge Robert McAlpin "three-legged Willie" Williamson holding court in 1837 under a live oak tree near where the first Colorado County courthouse was built. In 1838, lumber was cut in Bastrop and floated down the Colorado River for a courthouse that was to be built. Unfortunately, strong currents caused a barrier that had been constructed to stop the logs to fail, and the lumber continued down the Colorado River and was lost. After using rented spaces for over 10 years, the first courthouse was finally completed in 1848 or 1849. The second courthouse was built in 1857 of locally mixed concrete walls, and the third and final one in 1890 of stone and brick construction. The original roof on the third courthouse was destroyed by the hurricane of July 1909. When rebuilt, the clock tower was replaced with a dome using the original clocks to minimize costs. According to the Historic American Buildings Survey by the National Park Service in 1993, the courthouse is "an excellent example of an evolution of stylistic trends and has represented the focal point for Colorado County civic life for over one hundred years."

The position of city marshal of Columbus was abolished in 1903 as a result of the Colorado County Feud causing the position of county sheriff to become even more important in keeping the peace. The Colorado County Jail also played an important role in keeping criminals away from the good citizens living in and around Columbus.

According to legend, Judge Robert McAlpin "three-legged Willie" Williamson convened the first district court in Colorado County under one of the many oaks near the site of the present-day courthouse. This photograph of the Court Oak shows the historical plaque affixed to the tree with the courthouse in the background. Another account describes the judge's brief visit, probably on April 3, 1837, as being held in Nicholas Dillard's old schoolhouse near the river. He apparently heard no cases that day but made a speech asserting the authority of the just established court. He did, however, impose fines on several men who had been called to serve on the grand jury but declined to attend court. Judge Williamson was known as "three-legged Willie" because when he was 15 years old, he contracted an illness that confined him to his home for two years and left him a cripple for life. His right leg was drawn back at the knee; the wooden leg that he wore from the knee to the ground gave him his widely-known title.

The second Colorado County Courthouse, pictured here, was built in 1857 on the courthouse square in Columbus but was later demolished in 1890. This courthouse was built of a mixture of sand, gravel, and burnt lime. The mixture was poured into a form and left to harden to make a wall. Stucco was applied to the exterior for protection from the weather.

The third Colorado County Courthouse was built in 1890 by prominent Texas architect Eugene T. Heiner. This photograph shows the courthouse as it was originally built before a hurricane destroyed the clock tower and roof. Courthouse square is bounded by Walnut Street on the north, Travis Street on the east, Spring Street on the south, and Milam Street on the east.

Houston architect F.S. Glover's design for the replacement roof and clock tower destroyed by a hurricane in 1909 consisted of a round Classical Revival copper dome with the drum rising from a square base. A clear glass skylight was at the center of the dome. The gable ends each have a prominent pediment atop the entire gable with dentils on the pediment and cornice.

The crepe myrtle trees on the courthouse square were planted on November 11, 1919, in memory of those killed in World War I. Other vegetation on the courthouse square includes magnolia trees planted around the perimeter in 1905, 1907, and 1919, and pecan trees from the Pearfield Nursery planted along the hedge that surrounded the courthouse in 1925.

The 1882 iron fence that encircled the courthouse square was removed in November 1942 and was sold as scrap to help the war effort.

A stained glass dome covers the district court. It was covered with an acoustical tile ceiling in 1960 because of falling glass. Winds from Hurricane Carla in 1961 caused considerable damage to the dome and roof, making more repairs necessary, but the stained glass dome was not uncovered at that time. The stained glass was later uncovered and repaired in 1978 under the direction of local designer Arthur J. Willrodt.

Deputy Bob Kollmann (left) and Sheriff Sam Houston Reese are shown just after returning from hunting a fugitive in the 1890s. Reese was killed by Mark Townsend, Will Clements, and Marion Hope (brother of Larkin Hope, an earlier casualty of the Colorado County Feud) on March 16, 1899. Witness statements indicated that Reese provoked the gunfight, but his sons vowed revenge. The feud lasted from about 1898 to 1907.

This photograph shows the third Colorado County Jail as viewed from the southeast with the east bridge visible in the background. It was photographed in the 1930s, probably by Oscar Zumwalt, and used in the 1935 brochure *Columbus, Texas*.

The third Colorado County Jail was built in 1891. This photograph was taken around 1910.

Walter Eldridge Bridge was sheriff during the resurgence of the feud that involved the Staffords, Townsends, Reeses, and other families in the Columbus area. The position of city marshal was abolished in 1903, but an increase in killings associated with the feud caused the citizens to petition the city government to reestablish the position; they refused. County Judge Joseph Jefferson Mansfield then ordered an election that would unincorporate the town. The county took over the operation of the city government until Columbus was incorporated again in 1927.

Sheriff Frank Fred Hoegemeyer (left) and Deputy Barry Lenard Townsend are seen standing in front of the third Colorado County Jail in 1933.

The fourth Colorado County Jail opened in 1941. This photograph was taken around 1942 with Sheriff Harvey Lee, his family, and staff standing at the entrance. It was demolished in 1997 when the new jail was built on the western edge of Columbus near the Highway 71 bypass.

In 1896, the Colorado County officials were, from left to right, (seated) unidentified and County Judge Joseph Jefferson Mansfield; (standing) unidentified, Sheriff Sam Houston Reese, unidentified, and County Commissioner John Hastedt of Frelsburg. The other commissioners at the time were William Schoellmann of Nada, W.A. Van Alstyne of Weimar, and J.P. Anderson of Eagle Lake.

The Colorado County officials in 1902 were, from left to right, Walter Williams, commissioner for Weimar; Henry Thomas, commissioner for Columbus; J.J. Mansfield, county judge; Walter Eldridge "Dick" Bridge, sheriff; John Hastedt Sr., commissioner for Frelsburg; and ? Roberts, commissioner for Eagle Lake.

This portrait of Joseph Jefferson Mansfield was taken around 1930. He had a long and distinguished political career, serving as city attorney and mayor of Eagle Lake, county attorney and county judge of Colorado County, and US congressman from 1917 until his death in 1947. In 1921, he became ill and was confined to his bed for the next several months. When he returned to his duties in Washington in 1922, he was in a wheelchair and never walked again. Mansfield was chairman of the House Rivers and Harbors Committee in 1931. He secured key federal funding and worked closely with the people who created and managed the Lower Colorado River Authority (LCRA). In 1941, the Marshall Ford Dam was renamed Mansfield Dam in his honor. In the photograph below, Lyndon Baines Johnson is shown crouching next to Mansfield.

Six

FOOD FOR THE SOUL

As part of the contract that Stephen F. Austin had with the Mexican government, only the Catholic religion could be practiced in Texas. Consequently, Austin prohibited organized Protestant worship by his colonists. Though various Protestant Church histories list preachers conducting church services as early as 1824, they were held in private homes. Since there were not enough Catholic priests to service all the parishes in Texas, most communities did not have regular religious services. After Texas won its independence from Mexico in 1836, the Irish American immigrants in Texas petitioned the American church to send priests to the area. With the influx of French and German immigrants, there was also a need for multilingual priests.

Once Texas was independent of Mexico, the prohibition against the Protestant religion was lifted. Ordained ministers from the United States came to Texas to organize churches of various denominations. The Protestants who had been practicing their religion in small groups were now free to organize and build churches. The Lutherans organized their first church in the Columbus area in 1839. The Methodists were forming their churches at about the same time, though the earliest Methodist preacher was in the area in 1824. The first services of the Episcopal Church were believed to be held in Columbus in 1848 by Rev. Henry Niles Pierce, a missionary for Washington County. The first Baptist Church in Columbus was founded in 1855, though there was a report to the Texas Baptist Convention of a Sunday school in Columbus soon after Texas won its independence. Camp meetings were also being held in the area by the Methodists in the late 1840s. These events, at temporary sites with attendees staying overnight in tents, continued into the late 1800s.

While establishing religion and churches around Columbus was not an easy or linear process, it did succeed. Columbus and Alleyton have active churches that were established in the 19th century and others that were established throughout the 20th century. The Colorado County Historical Commission's *Colorado County Chronicles* was a valuable source of information about the churches in Columbus and Glidden.

Early Protestants in the Columbus area often did not have church buildings in which to worship. They would worship in each other's homes, under trees, in another church's building, or even in the courthouse. This photograph was taken around 1900 and shows a baptism in the Colorado River. It is probably near the East River Bridge.

After the death of his mentor, pastor, and friend Rev. Gusta Booker Sr., Rev. Carl Evans was led to found a church in memory of him in the mid-1960s. The result was the Booker Memorial Temple Church of God in Christ in Columbus. In the photograph at right, Evans can be seen preaching at the podium. The photograph below shows the church as it appears today. The church has been host to many state and local dignitaries, such as state representative John Wilson, Texas Attorney General John Hill, Laura Ann Rau, Charlie Phillips, Gusta Booker Jr., Gloria Barnes, and Theresa Fitzgerald.

St. Paul United Methodist Church is one of two Methodist churches in Columbus.

This photograph taken in August 1978 is of Lottie Davis with three children, Peter, Tracy, and Jon Swearingen. It was taken in front of New Greater Smith Chapel Baptist Church in Columbus.

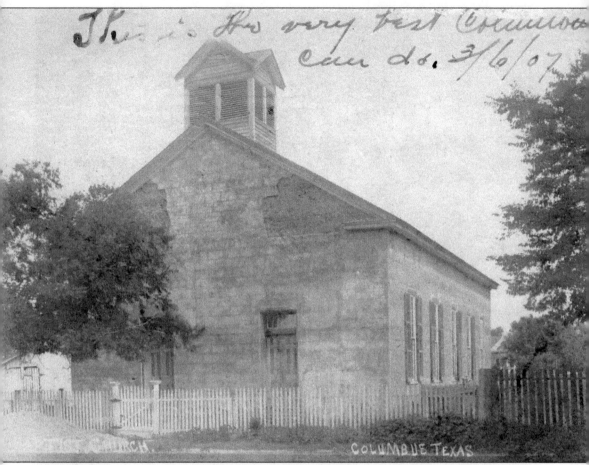

The First Baptist Church of Columbus was founded in 1855. By 1859, there were 38 white members and three black members. This photograph from 1930 shows the first church building that was constructed in 1860; it was known as the "concrete church" and was located on the corner of Live Oak and Washington Streets. It had the largest auditorium in town and was often used by other denominations and organizations.

This photograph shows the First Baptist Church built in 1909 while still under construction. It was wrecked in the 1909 hurricane that devastated Columbus and the congregation struggled to complete it. It was situated on the northwest corner of Walnut and Travis Streets. At the turn of the century, membership ranged between 95 and 100.

The completed First Baptist Church, Columbus, was photographed around 1913. The *Colorado Citizen* office is visible on the left, and the Live Oak Hotel can be seen behind it. The church building and hotel both were razed to build the Colorado County Federal Savings and Loan building, which is now Capital One Bank.

According to the Colorado County Historical Commission's *Colorado County Chronicles*, the first Catholic Church in Columbus was named St. Matthias and was built on land donated by the Tait family. A fire caused by a faulty flue destroyed a portion of the building in 1929. Instead of repairing the building, the parishioners decided to build a new church building. The Catholic Church Extension Society gave a large donation to this cause but requested that the name be changed to St. Anthony, which it was. The photograph at right is of Mt. Matthias Catholic Church in 1919. The photograph below is of the St. Anthony Catholic Church around 1930. It was photographed for use in the 1935 brochure *Columbus, Texas*.

The first record of a Lutheran church in Columbus was in 1839, when Rev. L.C. Ervendberg organized a congregation of six members. Until 1919 when St. Paul Lutheran Church was founded, Lutheran churches were organized and disbanded for various reasons. The Lutheran Ladies' Aid Society, formed in 1920, raised the money to buy land for St. Paul Lutheran Church. The photograph at left is from around 1930 and was used in the 1935 brochure *Columbus, Texas*. The photograph below was taken in 1965 of the charter members of St. Paul Lutheran Church with their pastor and his wife. Pictured are, from left to right, (seated) Anna E. Mattern, Eva Brandt, Emilia Stolle, Lizzie Brooks, William Brandt, and Owen Hoegemeyer; (standing) Pastor Harold L. Anderson, Mildred Anderson, H.C. Fowler, Ella Maples, Elsie Mattern, Raymond Fowler, Mrs. Sagebiel, and Dr. Sagebiel.

The first service of the Protestant Episcopal Church in Columbus is believed to have been held in 1848. Over the years, Episcopal services would be held in other churches and even the courthouse. St. John's Church was admitted into the diocese as a parish in April 1856. The church building pictured was built about 1874. It was extensively damaged in the 1909 storm that destroyed the clock tower on the courthouse. The church was repaired and moved to a more central location on the lot. This photograph was taken around 1930 and was used in the 1935 brochure *Columbus, Texas*. It was later used by the Church of Christ.

METHODIST CHURCH.
COLUMBUS TEXAS

According to the Colorado County Historical Commission's *Colorado County Chronicles*, Methodism started in Columbus with Henry Stephenson in June 1824. Small groups of colonists would gather on the river bank, under groves of trees, and in cabins to hear Stephenson and others preach. The Methodist Church seen here was built in 1897 and photographed around 1905. Since an early history gave the date of 1822 as the first formal organization of a Methodist Society, there was a Centenary Jubilee of Methodism and Protestantism held at the Columbus Methodist Church in 1922. It lasted for two days; the photograph below was taken of the celebration on October 6, 1922.

According to William Henry Harrison in *Alleyton, Texas: Backdoor to the Confederacy*, the first Protestant church built in Alleyton was in 1855; it was a satellite church organized by the Trinity Lutheran Church of Frelsburg. In May 1883, the *Colorado County Citizen* reported that the Alleyton Union Sunday school was reorganized with Dr. J.K. Davidson as superintendent. A Methodist Church was built sometime after 1885, but did not last. Trustees of the M.E. Church of Alleyton were deeded land in block 36 in 1878. Green Grove Baptist Church, organized in 1880, is the oldest still active church in Alleyton. Mt. Moriah Baptist Church, the second-oldest church that is still active, was organized in 1907. It is located next to the Alleyton Cemetery.

The Alleyton Church of Christ was organized in 1984 and is located on Camp Street.

Before the turn of the century, Christians in Glidden worshiped in each other's homes and later in the schoolhouse. The original plat of the town designated two lots in block 32 to be used for church purposes only. The group was composed of different denominations, but when put to a vote, the Baptists were in the majority. Subsequently, the Glidden Baptist Church was organized in November 1906. A building was built the next year, but it was destroyed in the 1909 storm. Another building was erected in 1910. That building was replaced by another that was constructed in the mid-1920s. This photograph was taken around 1930.

Seven

RAISING TOMORROW'S LEADERS

Before the formation of school districts by the Texas legislature in 1854, schools were governed by boards of trustees that were elected locally. Columbus established such schools in the early 1850s. Some of the most notable Columbus schools were the Colorado College (later Columbus High School), Columbus Female Seminary (Masonic), and the Columbus Seminary (boys only). When Columbus was disincorporated, the county commissioners took over control of the Columbus schools until the city was reincorporated in 1927.

In about 1885, St. Mary's Institute, established by the Sisters of Divine Providence, opened its doors in Columbus. It was a girl's school, but there is evidence that boys were also taught. The Sisters also operated the St. Matthias Parochial School in Columbus. They opened approximately 47 schools throughout Texas, and taught in both parochial and "free" schools in Colorado County.

According to *Alleyton, Texas: Back Door to the Confederacy* by William Henry Harrison, the earliest documented school in Alleyton was founded in 1871 with W.C. Wilson as the teacher. It overflowed by 1878, and became known as the Alleyton Male and Female School. It charged fees ranging from $1 to $5 per month depending upon the curriculum chosen. In 1907, an election was held to form the Alleyton Independent School District. In 1917, the Columbus Independent School District expanded and incorporated the Alleyton district into its system. Grades one through eight were kept in Alleyton in a one-room frame building at the corner of Harbert and Center Streets. In 1924, even this was permanently closed and students were bused to Columbus.

In 1895, Alice Townsend gave a one-half-acre tract of land to be used as a school in Glidden. Bettie Holt became Glidden's first teacher for the 1897–1898 school year. The people of Glidden built that first school. It was a one-room structure with windows only on the south side, and enclosed by a tall, white-painted wooden fence. There was a large gate for wagons, a turnstile for students, and a large stile over the top of the fence.

The earliest documented school in Alleyton was in 1871. In 1907, the Alleyton ISD was formed, but in 1917, the Columbus ISD expanded and incorporated Alleyton into its system. This photograph of the Alleyton School and students is from 1895. The one-room schoolhouse can be seen in the back.

This photograph of the Alleyton School and students is from March 1906. Pictured are, from left to right, (first row) Hillie Franz, unidentified, Walter Braden, Portia Gaedcke, Gilbert Gaedcke, unidentified, and Henry Gaedcke; (second row) Mattie Gillespie, Amy Walker, Kidder Walker, Colman Franz, Lillie Leesemann (teacher), Robert Prather, Willie Gillespie, Frank Potter, and Hardy Walker.

Pictured above are, from left to right, (first row) two unidentified girls, Anna Mae Harrison, unidentified, Margaret Everett, two unidentified girls, Laura Everett, and unidentified; (second row) two unidentified girls, Lille Leesemann (teacher), Hattie May Everett, and unidentified. All of the students in the back row are unidentified. The sign reads "Alleyton School." The below photograph from 1921 was one of the last taken at the Alleyton School since it was closed permanently in 1924. Alleyton students were sent to Columbus in a wagon that had chicken wire around the sides for their safety. When they reached the Columbus school, there would be a chorus of "here come the Alleyton chickens" to herald their arrival. The teacher shown here is Laura Everett.

Prior to 1895, when Alice Townsend gave land for a school building, children in Glidden were mostly taught at home, though some were sent away to school. According to *Come, Reminisce With Me: A History of Glidden, Texas, 1885–1985* by Dorothy Jean Heine, there was much excitement about Glidden's new school. Everyone worked together to get the buildings and grounds ready for school to begin in September. Like most schools of the time, the Glidden school used the McGuffey Reader series along with slate and chalk to practice writing and arithmetic. Spelling bees were held on Friday afternoons. Up until 1906, the school building was also used for church services. In 1908, a partition was added to accommodate the 65 students enrolled. The above photograph was taken in February 1914, and the photograph below is from 1929.

According to Barry A. Crouch's article in the *Nesbitt Memorial Library Journal*, the first official school opened by the Freedmen's Bureau in Columbus was in March 1866. Education was disrupted briefly during the yellow fever epidemic in the late summer of 1867. Both of these photographs of the Columbus Colored School were taken in 1930. The photograph of the building is taken from Preston Street. Willie Mae Axel can be seen holding a poster below. The teacher is Ora Lee Toland.

Colorado Academy Building was constructed in 1860 on Seminary Square, north of Jackson Street and south of Washington, between Live Oak and Bowie in Columbus. This was land given for the purpose of education by W.B. DeWees. The building was demolished in 1891. This photograph is one of a set of 20 made in Columbus in 1884 by Thomas B. Elrod and sent for exhibit to the New Orleans World Exposition. In December 1884, the *Colorado Citizen* referred to the building in this photograph as the college building.

This Columbus public school building replaced the original Colorado Academy building. Note the stile in front of the building that goes over the fence that surrounds the school. This school building was constructed in 1891 and was demolished around 1950. This photograph was taken around 1905.

A more modern high school was built in 1924. This photograph from 1930 was used in the 1935 brochure *Columbus, Texas*. As with the two previous buildings, it was built on Seminary Square on Washington Street between Bowie and Prairie. It was the first Columbus school building used strictly by the higher grades, and was demolished in the 1980s.

The St. Matthias Parochial School in Columbus was established by the Sisters of Divine Providence. The photograph above is from about 1885. In the top row, far right, is Charles Benjamin Stafford. All of the others are unidentified. According to the *Nesbitt Memorial Library Journal* in May 1992, a fire severely damaged the St. Matthias church building on March 2, 1929. The Catholic Church Extension Society donated a substantial amount of money towards the construction of a new facility with the condition that the parish be renamed in honor of St. Antony of Padua. In the photograph below, Clara Traylor is in the second row, fourth from the right, and Maude Alice Traylor is in the first row, fourth from the right. All others are unidentified.

One of the earliest photographs of Columbus students was taken in about 1880. Pictured are, from left to right, (first row) Daisy Yarbrough, Birdie Wesson, Myrtle Green, and Marcie Williard; (second row) Lillie Leeseman, Laura Rose, unidentified, Tracy Wagenfuhr, Fanny Jo Montgomery, Eva Wirtz, Nina Anderson, and Fannie Mahon; (third row) Logan Coffee, Lizzie Oakes, Lizzie Townsend, Lyda Boyd, Carrie Fitzgerald (teacher), May Harrison, Ida Chapman, Nina Anderson, and Ike Jones; (fourth row) Henry Montgomery, Lula Marst, John Stafford, Henrietta Weete, and Charley Riley. The second photograph of Columbus students is from 1888. The teacher is Kate Oakes. Seated in the second row, seventh from left is Etta McCormick. Others present are Maggie Mahon Ilse, Lillian Miller Ilse, Erma Zumwalt West, and Jesse Oaks; all others are unidentified.

Columbus students were photographed on April 26, 1895, on the front steps of the high school building. The teacher is Blanche Delaney. The boy in the dark shirt on the left in the back row is Albert Rau. The boy in the dark suit with the big white collar is Presley B. Mahon. Willis Youens is second from left in the second row. To the right of the teacher is Herman Paulsen. The girl in the black dress in the middle of the front row is Omi Thrower. Leona Welch is second from right in the first row. All others are unidentified. Notice that the boys are all barefoot and several of them are holding baseball bats. They seem ready for recess.

Times and school were different when these Columbus students posed for a photograph with their teachers in 1899. Pictured are, from left to right, (first row) Alvin Wirtz, Robert Wirtz, Foard Townsend, and Little Harrison; (second row) Frankie Dick, Bertha Wirtz, Leona Welch, Eva Harrison, Myrtle Farmer, Fay Burford, and Nina Welch; (third row) Sally Whitfield (teacher), Ned Burford, Lyle Logue, Joe Stafford, Seth Little, Eva Greenwood (teacher), and Grover Wagner.

In this Columbus High School class of 1912 photograph are, from left to right, (first row, seated) McBroom Vandiver Smith and Hazel Marion Hutchins; (second row, kneeling) Alice Elizabeth Burttschell; (third row) Lula Othelia Burttschell and unidentified; (fourth row) Clinton Harcourt Wooten, William Allen Holland, Glenn Errol Harbert, unidentified, and John Clyde Glithero.

Columbus seventh grade students were photographed on the steps of the school in November 1913. The teacher at rear is Helen Burttschell. The students are, from left to right, (first row) Bennie Waldvogel, Keene Cook, John White, Mark Hopkins, Henry Braden, and Ernest Gay; (second row) Blanche Eliot, Jacquelin Mansfield, Berta McDow, Ela Maxine Lessing, Laura Everett, Charline Glithero, Ouida Boulden, Esther Wegenhoft, Louise Andriano, Ona Mae Towell, and Jaley Perry.

This photograph of Columbus high school students was taken at the school in May 1921. Pictured are, from left to right, (first row) Thurmond West, Meteor Frnka, Frank Tait, Johnnie Hastedt, Dittman Harrison, Elbert Tait, Robert Burger, Lyle Farmer, and Louis Ramsey; (second row) Gladys Obenhaus, Phyrne Tanner, Ruby Grobe, Juanita Kearney, Vera Mayes, Lois Obenhaus, Johnie Lee Obenhaus, Jocelyn Hamburger, Mozelle Shaw, and David Jaloway; (third row) Margaret Hester, Lois Stafford, Cynthia Farmer, W.A. Holland (teacher), Mary Holland (teacher), Omi Thrower (teacher), Katy Mayes, JoMaude Brooks, Dora Goeppinger, Gisela Trojan, Geri Bowen, Eva Mae Heller, and Dorothy West; (fourth row) Lavigne Oakes, Dolly Heller, Lavelia Kirby, Margaret Everett, Lois Ricks, Lavenia Brandon, Willie Farrar Holland, and Douglas Richter; (fifth row) Arthur Nichols, Gene Baker, Robert Via, Sam Holland, Eddie Berger, Lavo Wegenhoft, and Frank Braden.

In 1930, a photograph of twin siblings in the Columbus school system was taken. Pictured are, from left to right, (first row) Mack and Jack Allen, Madeleine "Black-Eye" and Marceline "Blue-Eye" Schultz, and Alberta and Albert Schultz; (second row) Madeline and Adeline Hillmer, Clyde and Carl Fleming, and Jean and John Alley; (third row) Aileen and Elaine Lobpries, Ruby and Roxie Frnka, and Jewel and Burrell Burris.

As time went on, students at Columbus schools enjoyed extracurricular activities. This photograph shows the 1930 Columbus High School Orchestra. Members were Allen Brune, Edward Mattern, Robert Gillespie, Harry Tanner, William Henry Harrison, H.A. Ward Jr., Leah Wilson, Albert Ruhmann, Willie Mattern, Rose Pfeifer, Vivian Glithero, Roberta Struss, Ruby Struss, Catherine Skinner, Elizabeth Braden, Lillian Rutta, Minnie Pfeifer, J.L. Obenhaus, Evelyn Braden, and Mrs. Gus Streithoff, director.

The 1928 Columbus High School Pep Squad are, from left to right, (first row) Helen McMahon, Florence Cone, Virginia Goeppinger, and mascot Elizabeth Hahn; (second row) Myrtle Richardson, Isabel Fehrenkamp, Sammy Lee Austin, Lillian Hoegemeyer, Frances Adam, Mae Nichols, Lillian Sronce, Bernice Becica, WillieLee Hillmer, JoBeth Shaw, Ilse Miller, MaryElizabeth Youens, Elvira Leyendecker, Evelyn Frnka, and Leila Rau; (third row) Lova Schmidt, Helen Kelly, Joy Foster, Rosa Pfeifer, Evelyn Braden, Mildred Mayes, Kathryn Via, Eloise Hester, Gertrude Isgrig, Margaret Glithero, Henrietta Potter, Mary Litzmann, Helen Culpepper, and Winona Zwiegel.

In the 1959–1960 school year, the Columbus High School annual staff consisted of, from left to right, (seated) Helen David, Barbara Meismer, Margaret Scronce, Valena Koss, and Grace Lynton; (standing) Margaret Stavinoha, Barbara Jecmenek, Maybelle Cloat, Tommie Grissom, and Darla Gajeske. This photograph appeared in the 1960 Columbus High School yearbook, *The Cardinal.*

Many of the boys at Columbus High School were members of the Future Farmers of America. Each year, there was an FFA Fat Stock Show where they showed the animals they had raised. In 1959, Melvin "Butch" Meyer (holding trophy) won an award for the pig he had raised. Seen with him is LeRoy Stein. Liza McMahan is seated at the table behind Meyer.

Eight

WORK . . .

As with most of Texas, the area around Columbus was originally based on an agricultural economy. In Bill Stein's "Consider the Lily: The Ungilded History of Colorado County" published in the *Nesbitt Memorial Library Journal*, other than smithies, a German cigar factory established around 1840 was the first major industry around Columbus.

As time went on, however, other industries built up too; at first to support the agricultural economy, and later to survive on their own. Along with tobacco, cattle, and corn, cotton was the next major industry and primary cash crop to develop. It spawned cotton gins and a cottonseed oil manufacturing plant. Later, large deposits of sand and gravel were discovered near Columbus and continued to be a source of prosperity even during the Great Depression in the 1930s, as road construction was made affordable by the inexpensive source of local gravel.

During this time, banks, dry goods stores, general stores, drug stores, and doctors also contributed to support the growing community. A downturn in the town's economy came during the infamous Stafford-Townsend Feud in the late 1800s and early 1900s, when good, respectable citizens left town for other cities to escape the violence in Columbus and the surrounding area. The town was disincorporated in the early 1900s and was not incorporated again until 1927. By the 1930s, Columbus had overcome the era of violence and had returned to being a friendly law-abiding community.

As in most small towns in Texas, banking was important to commerce in Columbus. The first bank in Columbus was founded in 1873 by James H. Simpson. Robert E. Stafford opened the R.E. Stafford & Co. Bank in 1882. This 1906 photograph shows that bank located in the 1886 Stafford Opera House. The water tower is shown in the foreground. The Columbus Academy can be seen in the background.

The First State Bank opened for business in 1913 in the Stafford Bank building at Spring and Milam Streets. In 1916, it moved to property previously owned by the Simpson Bank on the northwest corner of Walnut and Milam Streets. This photograph is of the First State Bank building that replaced the original Simpson building. The Colorado County Courthouse can be seen in the background.

Columbus State Bank was founded August 19, 1919, in an old building on the west side of the square. Construction for this masonry building on the southwest corner of Walnut and Milam Streets was started just a few months later in October 1919. The masonry was made of lime and gravel poured into forms. According to a paper written by William H. Harrison entitled "History of Banking in Colorado County, Texas," this bank was capitalized with $50,000. Its growth was good, and they declared a 100 percent stock dividend in January 1953 and again in January 1966. The photograph below shows the interior of the Columbus State Bank on opening day.

Oscar A. Zumwalt bought his drugstore in Columbus in 1898 from Ike Towell. It was originally opened in 1844 by Dr. John Logue. The photograph at left shows Ike Towell (in white shirt) and an unidentified man seated in front of Zumwalt's Drug Store around 1905. Zumwalt provided numerous photographs of the City of Columbus that were sold as postcards. In 1934, Towell decided he had lived long enough and killed himself with ether. In the below photograph are James H. and Mattie Caldwell on the south side of Davis Drug Store, another pharmacy in Columbus, during World War II. The Columbus Colored School can be seen in the background.

Diners were common in most towns in Texas. This photograph shows the interior of Burt Sandwich Shop in Columbus on July 21, 1949. Pictured are, from left to right, Georgia ?, Leroy Burt Jr., Essie Hammond, and Agnes Burt.

In addition to sit-down cafés or diners, prepared food could also be bought from street vendors. This photograph shows Hattie Ellis, the tamale lady, with her cart in the yard in Columbus. The sign on the cart reads "Hot Tamales 80¢ per doz."

Kuhn's Café was located in Glidden, which is just west of Columbus on Highway 90. Next door to the café was an establishment that offered alcoholic beverages, Dr. Pepper, and haircuts.

Brown News Café was located at the train depot in Glidden. This photograph shows the interior. None of the people are identified.

The Ehrenwerth-Ramsey-Untermeyer Building was built in 1873 by Henry M. Ehrenwerth for his mercantile store. It is made of bricks from a local kiln. It has also housed L.G. Smith's Red Elk Saloon and Gambling Hall in the 1880s and James Ramsey's hardware, implement, and undertaking business beginning in the mid-1890s. It was sold to the Untermeyer brothers in 1825 and used as a hardware store.

The Brick Store House, of locally made bricks, was built and occupied from 1850 to 1867 by Thomas W. Harris, a physician from Virginia. It was later bought by William and Mary Pinchback in 1867, Bertha Wagner in 1878, and was owned by Wagner heirs for about 100 years. From 1912 until the 1970s it housed Fehrenkamp Grocery. Being the oldest commercial building left standing in Columbus, it is a recorded Texas Historic Landmark.

The Stein-Heller Store was located on Milam Street in Columbus. It was constructed in the 1890s. Seen above is the interior of the store in 1912. Pictured are, from left to right, Erb Winn, Joe Heller, and Placide Heller. In Alleyton, Charles August Dittman was the proprietor of C.A. Dittman General Merchandise Store, seen below. This photograph is from 1892. Pictured are, from left to right, (with bicycles) Luella McLeod, Henry Dittman, and Bettie Pauline Dittman. C.A. Dittman is the father of the Dittman children. In the wagon is H.C. Gaedke. On the porch are, from left to right, an unidentified man, Andrew Alley, Berthold Leysaht (store manager), an unidentified child, two unidentified women, an unidentified man, and Otis Finney (with tall boots). The rest of the people on the porch are unidentified. The identifications are courtesy of William Henry Harrison's book *Alleyton, Texas: Back Door to the Confederacy*.

In February 1913, the Everett brothers, James John and Laban Tarleton, bought the general store in Alleyton from T.W. McLeod. The photograph at right is of McLeod's last visit to his store. Pictured are, from left to right, Hugh Wilson, James John Everett, T.W. McLeod, and Laban Tarleton Everett. In December of that same year, a flood on the Colorado River damaged the building. The Everett brothers rebuilt on the same location, adding a concrete porch. Later, gasoline was also sold. The photograph below was taken in the early 1940s and shows two of the patrons of the store. In 1949, the Alleyton Post Office was moved from the Hennicke store to this location. Margaret Everett Griffith was the first post mistress after it moved. (Right, courtesy of Lena Everett Kerr.)

Two other important commercial enterprises around Columbus were barbershops and funeral parlors. This photograph shows the interior of Emil J. Burger's barbershop on Milam Street between Crockett and Walnut Streets around 1920. The barber at rear center is Emil J. Burger. The others are unidentified.

This photograph of the Ben Davis Funeral Home was probably taken in the 1930s. This establishment still exists in Columbus in a different building.

The Brunson Building in Columbus was built in 1891 by Charles Brunson. He operated a saloon on the first floor. The second floor was a meeting hall until December 1896, when it was converted into the Lone Star Opera House. He added an adjacent store in 1896. Charles Brunson is the third man from the left. It now houses the Live Oak Art Center.

Ilse's Saloon was located down the street opposite the courthouse square. This photograph shows the interior in 1918. The patrons are, from left to right, F. Alley, August Ilse (behind bar), Arthur Leyendecker, Louis Schulenburg, Henry Ilse (behind bar), Albert Leyendecker, six unidentified men, Noonce Mahon, and four unidentified men.

Burt and Stafford Garage, built in 1919 by John Clemons Burt and Joe Walker Stafford, was on the northeast corner of Walnut and Bowie Streets in Columbus. It originally housed a Chevrolet automobile dealership. Charley Stafford is seen leaning on the "Stop Here" sign. All others are unidentified. The above photograph was taken in 1919. The photograph below shows the same building as the S.K. Seymour Hardware and Lumber Company. In later years, it was Simmons Lumber and today it houses AL&M Do It Best, a hardware store and lumberyard.

Columbus boasted an ample number of gas stations, mostly along Highway 90, also known as Walnut Street. This Texaco service station on the south side of Walnut Street was photographed in the 1930s. It is located near the East River Bridge. After enclosing the drive-thru area, it now houses Trimmer's Den.

The Magnolia Petroleum Co. sold Mobil gasoline and was located on the north side of Walnut Street near the East River Bridge. It was across the street from the gas station shown in the photograph above. This photograph was taken around 1940 from the east. The building is still standing. The legal row, which housed various legal offices, can be seen to the left of the station.

The Tolbirt Garage can be seen in this 1925 photograph. It was located on the southwest corner of Milam and Spring Streets. The Columbus State Bank drive-thru is now at that location. The Stafford Opera House can be seen in the background.

Columbus, Texas Meat & Ice Company was built in 1884 on the north side of Robson Street, at the site of Robson's Castle, between Fannin and Austin in Columbus. It was one of three packing houses in Texas. Established to process at place of origin, the plant could handle 125 cattle per day. Some of its beef was sent to London. Robert E. Stafford was the major stockholder. The photograph is one of a set of 20 made in Columbus in 1884 by Thomas B. Elrod and sent for exhibit to the New Orleans World Exposition.

This view of downtown Columbus was taken from the top of the courthouse around 1910. It shows legal row on Walnut Street in the lower left corner and the buildings along Milam Street between Walnut and Crockett Streets.

Downtown Columbus, with the corner of Walnut and Milam Streets at the lower right, was photographed from atop the water tower. It is one of a set of 20 photographs made in Columbus in 1884 by Thomas B. Elrod and sent for exhibit to the New Orleans World Exposition. On December 4, 1884, *The Colorado Citizen* referred to this photograph as "Manufacturing Quarter, North."

This photograph from the 1930s shows Milam Street in downtown Columbus. It is of the storefronts on the west side of the street between Walnut and Crockett Streets. On the left side of the street, the establishments of D.G. Boyd and the Nesbitt Pharmacy can be seen. Past the D.G. Boyd building, the Brunson Building can be seen, which now houses the Live Oak Art Center. On the right, a sign for Central Power and Light Company can barely be seen.

Hospitals and doctors provided the medical attention that was so important to a growing community. There were three Dr. Robert Henry Harrisons in Colorado County. Two were in Columbus, both going by Dr. R.H. Harrison—"old Dr. Bob" and "young Dr. Bob," and the third practiced in Alleyton, going by Dr. R. Henry Harrison or "little Bob." The Galveston, Harrisburg & San Antonio Railroad Hospital, founded by "old Dr. Bob," was converted from a hotel to a hospital in 1880. It was on the north side of Spring Street, between Bowie and Live Oak Streets in Columbus. The building with the porch was the hospital. The smaller building in the rear was a two-story bathhouse, which was added in 1885. The complex burned in June 1887. The photograph is one of a set of 20 made in Columbus in 1884 by Thomas B. Elrod and sent for exhibit to the New Orleans World Exposition. On December 4, 1884, the *Colorado Citizen* referred to this photograph as "G.H. & S.A. Hospital."

"Old Dr. Bob's" (Dr. Robert Henry Harrison) home, with Harrison pictured in an inset, was built in the 1870s on the corner of Preston and Front Streets in Columbus. It was destroyed by fire in August 1915. The photograph is one of a set of 20 made in Columbus in 1884 by Thomas B. Elrod and sent for exhibit to the New Orleans World Exposition. Below, Dr. R. Henry "little Bob" Harrison's drug store, bought from Dr. W.L. Davidson in Alleyton, is shown. On the porch are Alleyton residents Laban Tarleton Everett, H.C. Gaedke Jr., and William Dittman.

After Dr. Robert Henry "old Dr. Bob" Harrison's hospital burned in 1887, Columbus was without a hospital for 44 years. The John F. Bell Memorial Hospital was built by Robert Harvey Bell, MD, in 1937. The above photograph was taken soon after its construction. The name was later changed to Columbus Hospital when Dr. Bell sold it to Clarence Irwin Shult, MD, after World War II. James Harbert Wooten Jr., MD, accepted a partnership from Shult in 1945, at which time the building was remodeled and enlarged to accommodate the two physicians. At that time, the name was changed to Columbus Hospital and Clinic. The photograph below is of the same building with the additions in 1947.

To accommodate the traveling public and those who were unable to sustain a private home, hotels became an important part of the community. Since Columbus was on the railroad line between Los Angeles and Houston, it was an easy destination. This photograph shows the Mayes Hotel in April 1837; it was torn down in July 2011. The Court Oak, where it is reported that the first district court in the county was held, can be seen in the middle of the street.

This photograph of the Hotel Colorado was taken around 1970. It is located on Milam Street between Crockett and Preston Streets in Columbus. It was repurposed in 1999 as the Home Design Studio & Gifts.

This photograph, taken by pharmacist Oscar A. Zumwalt, shows the Kulow Hotel in Columbus around 1910. According to the *Nesbitt Memorial Library Journal* by editor Bill Stein, the hotel was built by Helmuth Kulow in 1883, near the railroad depot in Columbus. It was his desire to create a first class hotel in the town, and it was built at a cost in excess of $1,000.

According to information in the *Nesbitt Memorial Library Journal*, the Live Oak Hotel in Columbus faced the railroad depot. The old Baptist Church on Walnut Street (US Highway 90) backed up to the hotel at the rear. Most of the guests were salesmen who had arrived on the train. This photograph was taken in the 1930s and was used in the 1935 brochure *Columbus, Texas*.

The early settlers to the county brought with them the agricultural practices they knew. Cotton was a crop they knew. In the early days, growing cotton was labor intensive, and the families as well as hired help were used to gather the cotton during the harvest. However, as improved machinery became available, the cotton farmers took advantage of it. The market for the cotton grown in Colorado County was historically foreign. Since there has been an increase in cotton grown abroad, the demand has dropped domestically; consequently, very little cotton is grown in the county today. Cotton farming was replaced by rice farming in many places. These photographs were taken around 1910 and 1920.

The invention of the cotton gin by Eli Whitney in 1794 greatly sped the growing of cotton and the cotton industry. The first cotton gin appeared in Texas in 1825; soon there were gins in most of the towns. This photograph shows the Towell and Shaw Cotton Gin at Columbus in September 1910. Standing in the foreground are Joe Shaw (left) and Jim Towell.

In the early years, cotton was transported to the gin by wagon; the cotton in this wagon was raised by James John Everett of Alleyton and photographed on September 13, 1912. Notice that the front wheel is smaller than the back wheel. This was because the front wheels were used to turn the wagon, and having a smaller wheel in front decreased the turning radius without the wheels hitting the wagon.

The area around Columbus contains large gravel deposits. The gravel industry was a major part of the economy in Colorado County throughout most of the 20th century and continues in the 21st century. While the strip mining of gravel could create unsightly terrain, the industry also allowed landowners to retain their land during the Great Depression. This photograph shows a Texas Construction Materials dragline near Alleyton on June 20, 1930.

It was necessary to build railroad lines to the pits to transport the gravel to market. This photograph shows the laying of Laban Spur No. 1 to a gravel pit at Alleyton in June 1930. Pictured are, from left to right, Luther Sylvester Lawrence, Laban Talbot Everett, two unidentified men, Maud McMahon McDow, Margaret Everett Griffith, and 11 unidentified men.

In May 1929, Gemmer & Tanner merged with Beaumont Building Materials Co. and formed Texas Construction Materials Co. (TCM). Soon after, the Columbus Gravel Co. also merged with TCM. TCM maintained offices and a complete machine shop on the old BBB&C Railroad right-of-way on Center Street in Alleyton. From there, gravel was shipped from the Everett Bros. gravel pit just south of the office to contractors in Houston. Both were closed when the supply of gravel in the area was exhausted. The above photograph shows railroad men employed by the company in 1932. The man at the far left is section foreman for Gemmer & Tanner, Pete Ruiz. The photograph below shows a Gemmer & Tanner Company dragline in 1932.

The early farmers used the rich land near creek and river bottoms to plant, and felt the rest was only suitable for grazing cattle. With the increasing population in the area, demand for farm goods increased. To meet the demand, the farmers began encroaching on the grazing land. Cattlemen found it advantageous to find and develop better herds of cattle that produced more and better quality meat from smaller acreages of land. The Longhorn cattle began to disappear, replaced by Herefords and Brahmas. The Brahmas proved suitable for the hot Texas climate, but in later years the Herefords, originally from England, have been phased out in favor of other breeds of cattle. The above photograph shows cattle dipping at the Tait Ranch in 1949. The photograph below was taken on the Wooten Ranch near Columbus.

Nine

... AND PLAY

Enjoyable pastimes have always been a part of life in Columbus. This chapter explores activities that bring the Columbus community together. These include activities of the volunteer fire department, community celebrations, birthday parties, canoeing, bicycling, sports, the Magnolia Belles, the Stafford Opera House, rodeos, the county fair, and other activities.

The earliest known Columbus Volunteer Fire Department chief was Dave Steiner in 1886. Since then, the volunteer fire department has not only protected the citizens of Columbus, but has actively engaged in community activities. The Colorado County Fair originated with the Volks Fest in 1872. The fair moved to its current fair grounds in 1978, and continues to be a premier local event. The annual cemetery tour sponsored by the Nesbitt Library Foundation originated in 2003 and has become a favorite activity for local residents, as well as the entire area. Under the auspices of the Columbus Historical Preservation Trust, the 1886 Stafford Opera House has held a very popular annual series of dinner theater events since 1998.

The Magnolia Homes Tour, with the Magnolia Belles as hostesses, was an annual event that opened up homes with a unique history or architectural style to the public. The Dilue Rose Harris House, the Brandon House, and the Alley Log Cabin, which are under the care of the Columbus Historical Preservation Trust, have been perennial favorites on the tour.

Beeson's Park, which was created by the Lower Colorado River Authority, has resulted in a common gathering point for picnics, soccer games, bicycling events, and political speeches. It also provides boating access to the Colorado River.

While the Columbus Volunteer Fire Department has a very serious purpose, they are also noted for having a good time. In the above photograph, the Columbus Fire Company in conjunction with the Columbus Cornet Band is greeting the train of gubernatorial candidate John C. Ireland in July 1882. In the photograph below from the 1890s, uniformed band members are posed on the courthouse square. They are, from left to right, (first row) John Trojan, Arnold Trojan, Leo Kohleffel, Eddie Gloger, unidentified, Frank Stuppel, Wenzel Frank Zwiener, Emil Burger, Charles Zwiener, and Henry Senftenberg; (second row) unidentified, Ed Matzke, Gus Depmore, Joe Juenger, unidentified, A. Bartles, and A. Scholandt. The rest are unidentified.

On June 19, 1865, Gen. Gordon Granger issued a general order in Galveston, freeing the quarter million slaves in Texas. The Juneteenth celebration commemorates that day. Texas is the only state in which Juneteenth is a legal holiday. This c. 1910 photograph shows a Juneteenth celebration in Columbus. The 1879 Juneteenth celebration attracted an estimated 600 people.

The caption on this photograph reads, "That Good Old Dinner Time." Crowds of people are eating at tables at the 1909 Colorado County Fair, with the Eagle Lake sugar cane exhibit visible in the background. On November 1, 1909, Charles Nagel, secretary of commerce and labor under President Taft, addressed the 1909 fair. New fairgrounds were established in Columbus in 1978, and the fair has continued to be a very popular annual event.

Jocelyn Hamburger's birthday party was held on the courthouse square on July 26, 1908. Jocelyn was the daughter of Sam Hamburger, who owned a local clothing store. He was also on the Republican State Executive Committee for several years. Sam was an orthodox Jew and when he would leave town, his wife, Ida, would immediately start eating some of her favorite foods—bacon and chitlins (pig intestines). Jocelyn married a dentist from Dallas.

Jack Hillmer's birthday party in 1920 took place at the Live Oak Hotel that was owned by his mother near the passenger depot. Pictured here are, from left to right, (first row) two unidentified children, Clarence Geiselman, Jack Hillmer, Grace Adam, Tommy Allen, and Margaret Wirtz; (second row) Frances Adam, Russell Lowrey, Henri Lynn Buescher, Vera Jewel Wegenhoft, Kathryn Via, unidentified, Sam Harbert, Mildred Mayes, and Nina Via. Jack Hillmer became a renowned architect in California. His homes were featured in *Life Magazine* and the San Francisco Museum of Art.

The Colorado River has always provided opportunities for water sports. This early 1900s photograph is of a swimming hole, probably near the north bridge in Columbus. Both men and women are shown in swimwear that is consistent with other pictures from 1910 to 1920. The river appears to be very slow-moving.

Canoeing has also been popular on the Colorado River. The large bend in the river permits access north of Columbus, and after going downstream for 11 or 12 miles, you arrive at Beeson's Park about two miles from the starting point. This photograph shows canoe race winners with Miss Columbus Julie Ruffeno in 1985.

Men and women have always had some different ideas with respect to enjoyable pastimes. In the above photograph, ladies are shown posing with canes in front of an automobile in 1925. Shown are Lucille Stein, Hazel Hutchins, unidentified, Margaret Mansfield, and unidentified. Below, some men are shown with their hunting trophy, a dead coyote, in 1918. The men are Charles Renz, John Batla, Joe Novosad, Joe Renz, and Adolph Renz. It is interesting to note that both groups are using a new symbol of affluence, the automobile, as their backdrop.

Alleyton seems to be the local area with the most alligators. Although not common, swimmers beware! The late 1940s photograph at right features Billie Gunn and Walter Dick with an alligator they killed at a nearby gravel pit. They are shown in front of the Everett Bros. Store in Alleyton. The 1957 photograph below shows a larger alligator, killed by Cunningham Leroy Griffith, on the side of the Everett Bros. Store in Alleyton. The man on the right is "Papa Sam" Williams. The three children in the foreground are, from left to right, Marilyn Brasher (Wade), Mike Brasher, and Ross McDow. The girl touching the alligator is Ann Brasher (West).

The popularity of football in small Texas towns is well-known. Columbus is no exception. The Columbus Cardinals football team in 1935 included, from left to right, (backfield) Milton Schultz, Junior "Hub" Huebel, Robert Schiller, and T.W. "Cully" Culpepper; (linemen) Leon Schindler, Willis Youens, Albert Hahn, Peter Hahn, Leland Zatopek, Roy Gillette, and Tillman Meisel.

The Columbus High School basketball team won the December 1961 tournament in Weimar. They are, from left to right, Dickie Pate, Donnie Brune, Buddy Anderson, Billy Youens, Mike Mitchell, Ervin Mieth, Al Wayne Radke, Tom Hancher, Jim Hastedt, Karl Youens, and Clay Doyle, superintendent of the Weimar Public Schools.

The 1895 baseball team consisted of, from left to right, (first row) Leo Hahn, Charley Stafford, and Lavo Hester; (second row) unidentified, Joe Stafford, and Henry Hahn; (third row) Ed Sandmeyer, Ed Goldsmith, Albert Hahn, unidentified, and Keity Wallace. The earliest recorded baseball game in Colorado County was held at the Volks Fest in 1872, when the Pioneer Baseball Club beat the Columbus Baseball Club. The unusual 1898 baseball photograph, shown here, was taken by L. Eugene Delfraisse in a photographer's studio. Charley Stafford is the man with the catcher's mitt. The other man is Lavo Hester.

The Caledonia Masonic Lodge No. 68 was formed in 1851 and has been active in the community ever since. This 1950s photograph shows an inspection of Knights Templar at the Columbus Masonic Lodge. Pictured are, from left to right, (first row) Otto P. Moore Jr., Marvin Hillmer, Boyd Smith, Nat Goodwin, unidentified, Elbert Cassell, A.D. "Sonny" Schumann, and unidentified (the inspector); (second row) John Busselmann, James D. Seymour Jr., Red Tolbirt, A.N. Evans Jr., and unidentified.

This photograph shows a float in the April 1960 Future Farmers of America parade in Columbus. They are, from left to right, Jan Hastedt, unidentified, Kenneth Wegenhoft, two unidentified, and Bernice Perry. The Future Farmers of America was founded in 1928 to support agricultural education. Their motto is "Learning to Do, Doing to Learn, Earning to Live, Living to Serve."

Entertainers at the 1969 Rotary Club Christmas Party are, from left to right, Samantha Echols, Angie Giddens, Mrs. Wayne Wolf, and Mary Hancher. The Rotary Club in Columbus was formed in 1937. The stated purpose of the organization is to bring together business and professional leaders to provide humanitarian service, encourage high ethical standards in all vocations, and help build goodwill and peace in the world.

The cast of the play *The Beauty Machine* is shown at the Stafford Opera House in Columbus in 1909. From left to right are Mrs. I.G. Stafford, Trula Harbert, Geraldine Gegenworth, Mrs. S. Simpson, Hazel Hutchins, Margaret Mansfield, Loraine Sandmeyer, Glenn Harbert, Lula Gegenworth, Fannie Rau, Alma Dick, Mrs. S.H. Simpson, J. Hamburger, Mrs. E.A. Hutchins (who played the queen), Mrs. E.S. Sandmeyer, Dorothy West, Ida Hamburger, Nell Sandmeyer, Martha Holt, Miss Wilson, Tracy Lielsdorf, Hannah Burger, Hattie Tait, Mary Seymour, Josie Shaw, Georgia B. McCane, and Carl Leesemann.

The Stafford Opera House was built in 1886. While not continuously used as an opera house, it has had a resurgence in recent years. *Sights and Sounds of Broadway* was presented in May 1984. The entertainers are Cathy Blymyer, Leslie Alford, Trisha Teltschick, Donna Defossas, Johanna Stallman McNutt, Brenda Marburger, Laura Cox, Ruth Terry, and Robin Meyer.

The Magnolia Belles are sponsored by the Columbus Historical Preservation Trust and act as hostesses for historical homes in Columbus. The May 1989 Belles are, from left to right, (first row) Natalie Barnett, Faith Lighthill, Stephanie Binford, Tammy Toepperwein, Kristie Barten, and Evelyn Gibson; (second row) Rebecca Anderson, Amy Elliot, Tina Kollmann, Leigh Hastedt, Pam Renz, and unidentified; (third row) Sharon Kubicek, Wanda Strey, Rachel Schonenburg, Jennifer Beaird, and Susan Self; (fourth row) three unidentified women, Cindy Pflughaupt, Ashley Ford, Lori Cloat, Christina Rogers, Stacie Glaeser, Patti Hopper, Jennifer Shoen, Valorie Perez, and Susan Siewert.

Ranching was the founding industry in Columbus and has always been an important part of local life. While the life of a rancher could be hard, there was always time for entertainment. This photograph shows Charles Renz performing a rope trick, "looping the loop," in 1910.

The rodeo parade through downtown Columbus on July 5, 1948, was photographed at the intersection of Milam and Walnut Streets. Fehrenkamp's Grocery, the oldest commercial building in Columbus, is visible in the background. The two boys in front are Doug and Bobbie Potter. Behind them are Edith and Bob Potter. Behind Edith Potter is Marley Giddens, and behind him to his right is Angie Giddens.

Visit us at
arcadiapublishing.com

Printed in the USA
CPSIA information can be obtained
at www.ICGtesting.com
LVHW071458041223
765647LV00008B/140